TRUCKS CARS AND PLANES

COLORING BOOK

by Ann Rainbow

Copyright © 2017 by Ann Rainbow

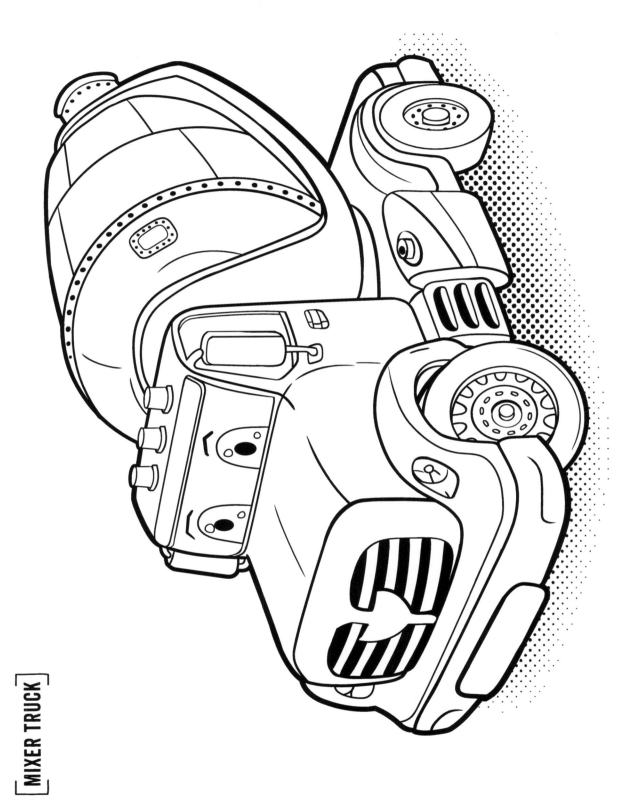

MIXER TRUCK

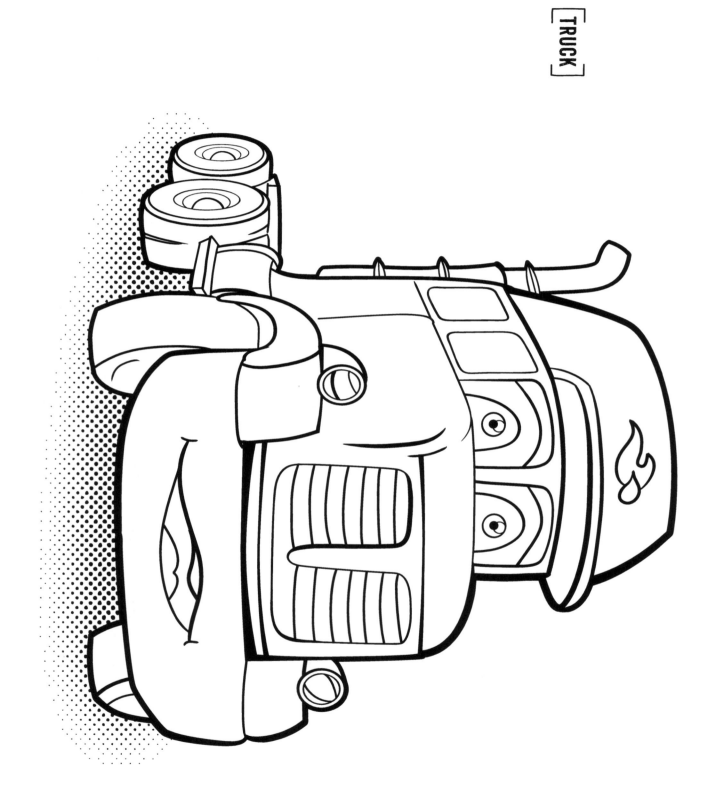

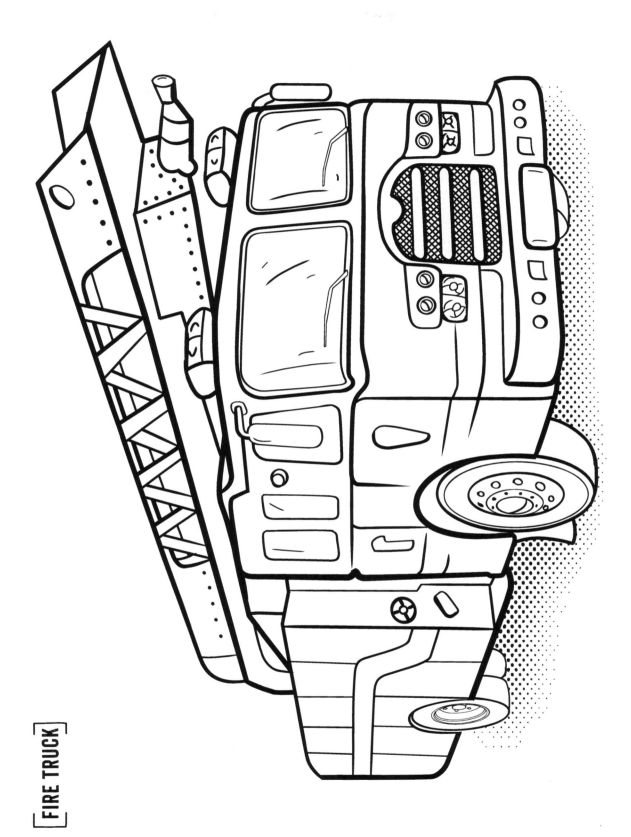

FIRE TRUCK

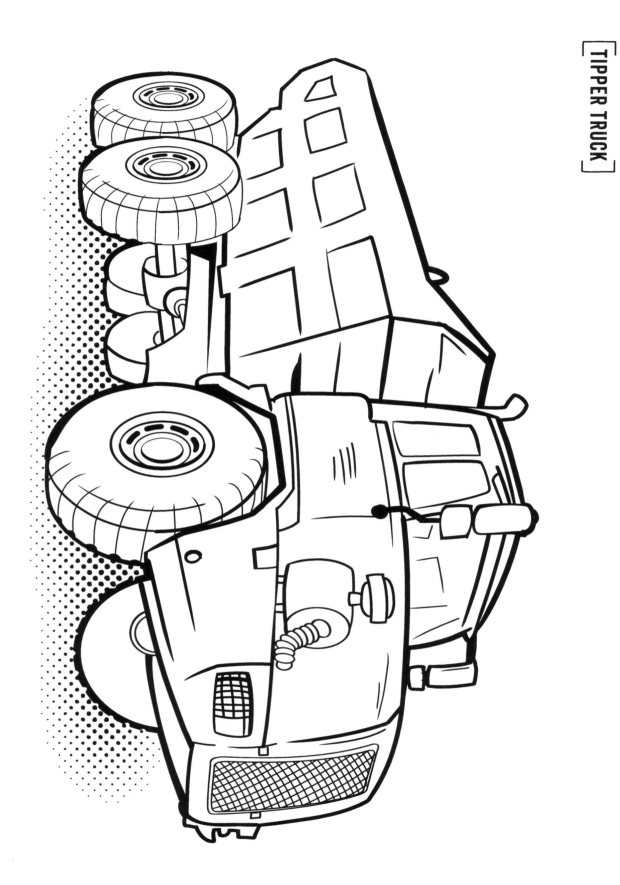

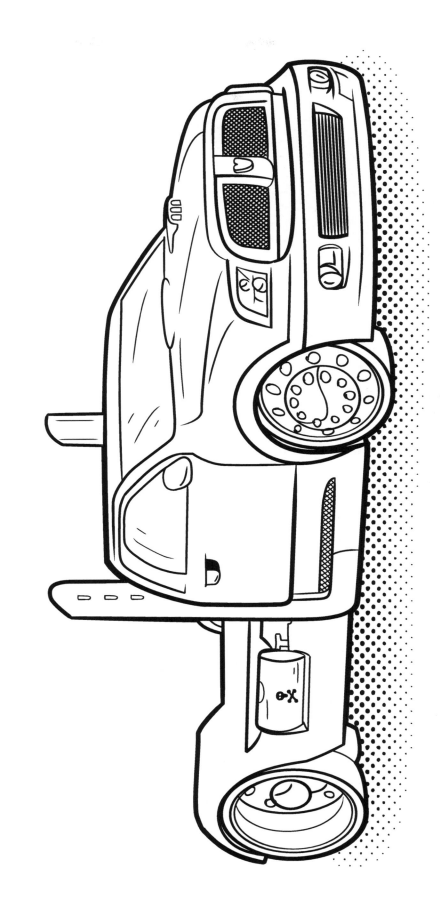

TRUCK

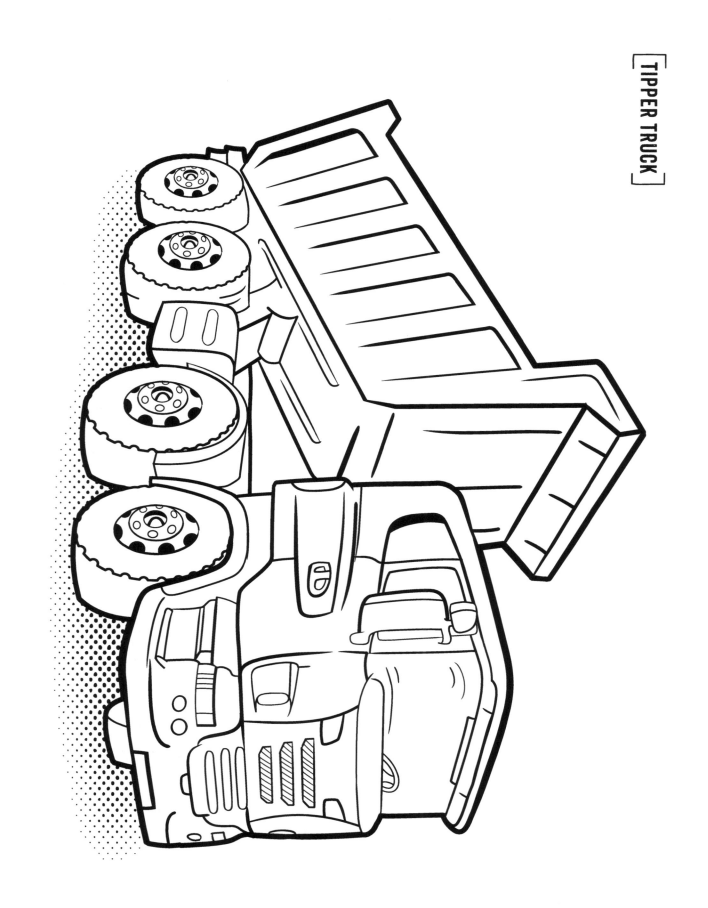

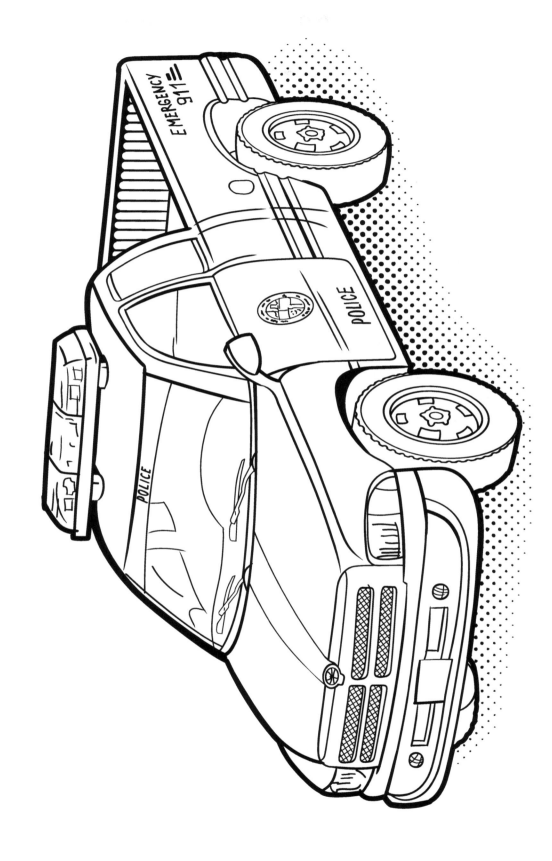

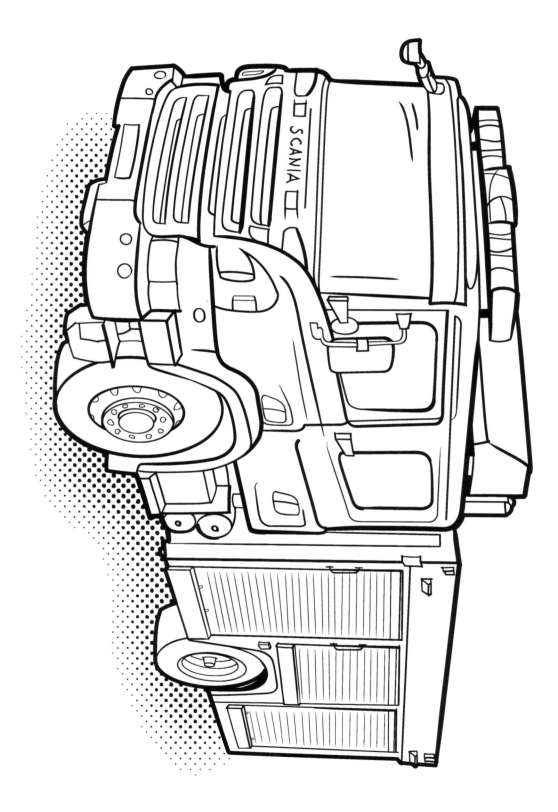

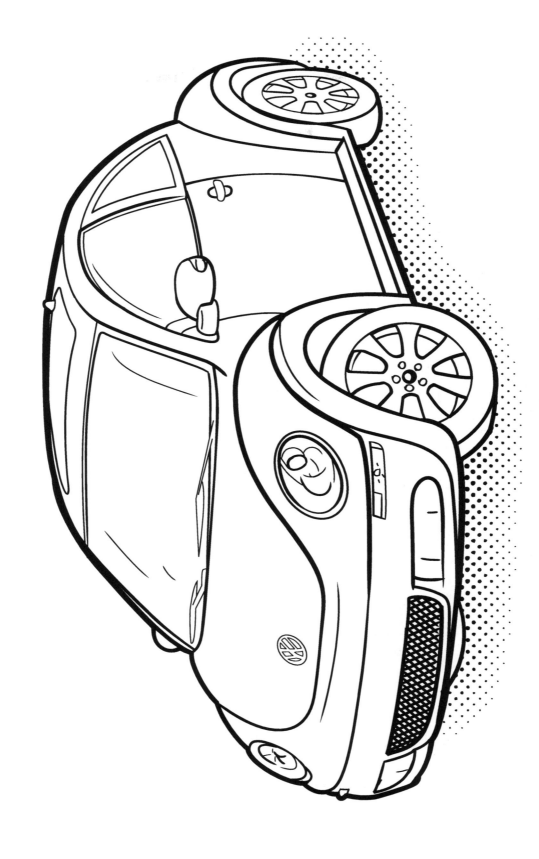

ICE CREAM TRUCK

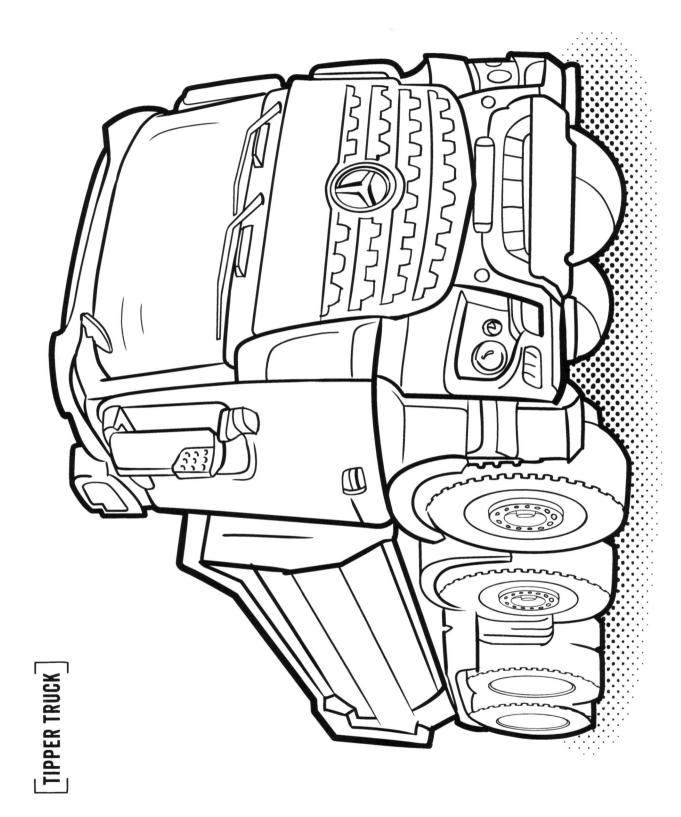

TIPPER TRUCK

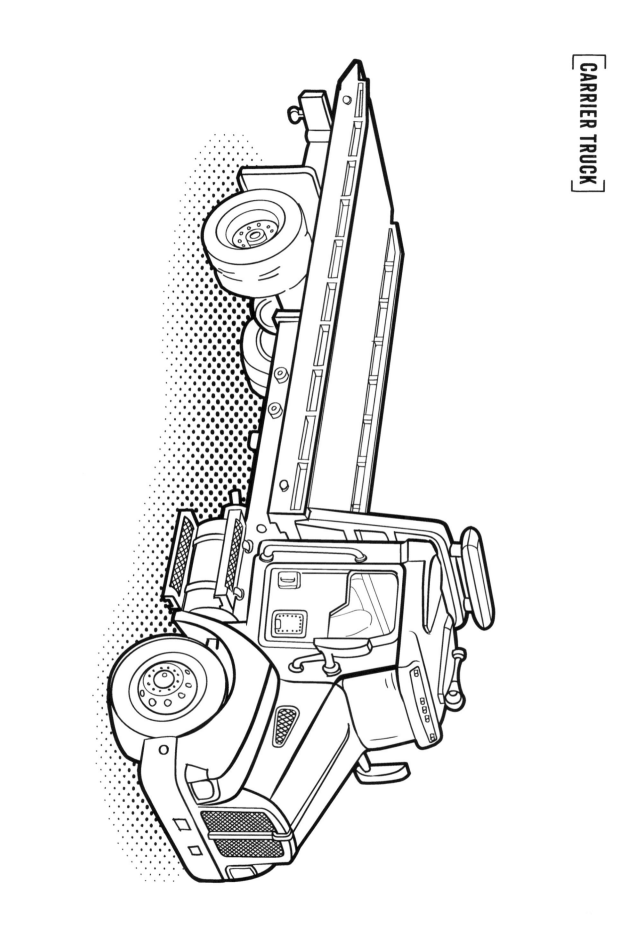

CARRIER TRUCK

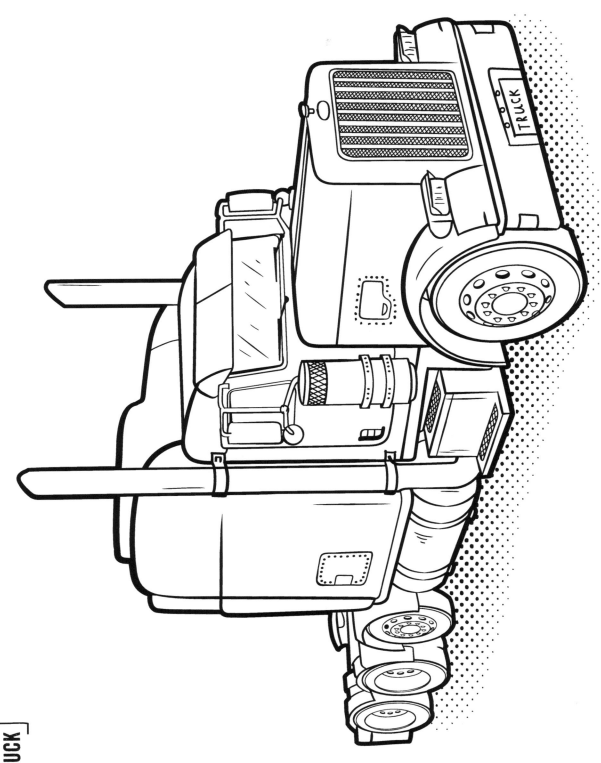

TRUCK

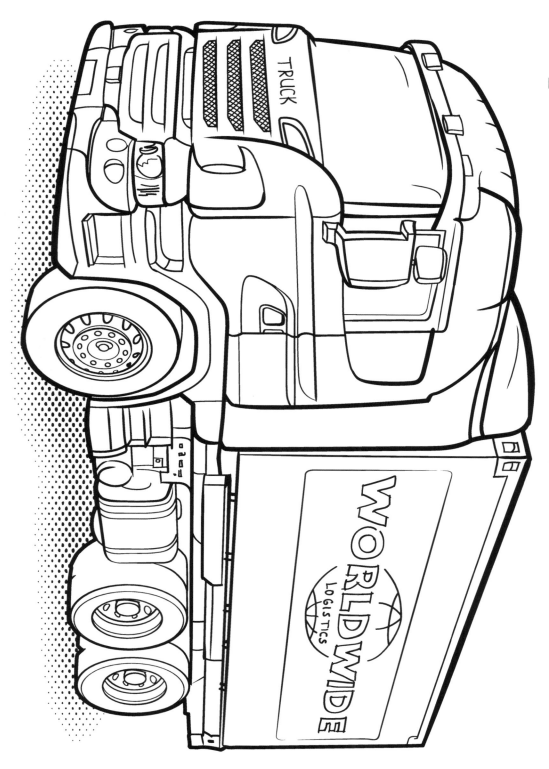

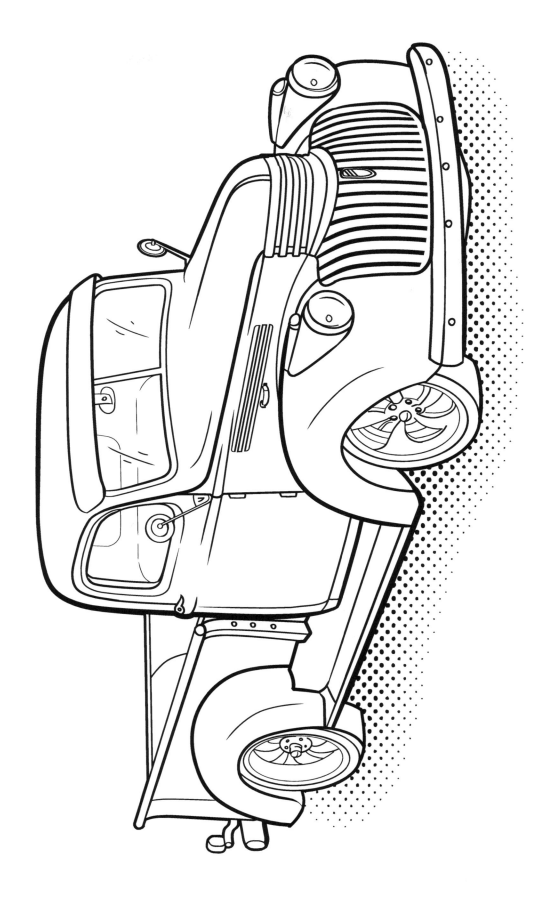

PICKUP TRUCK

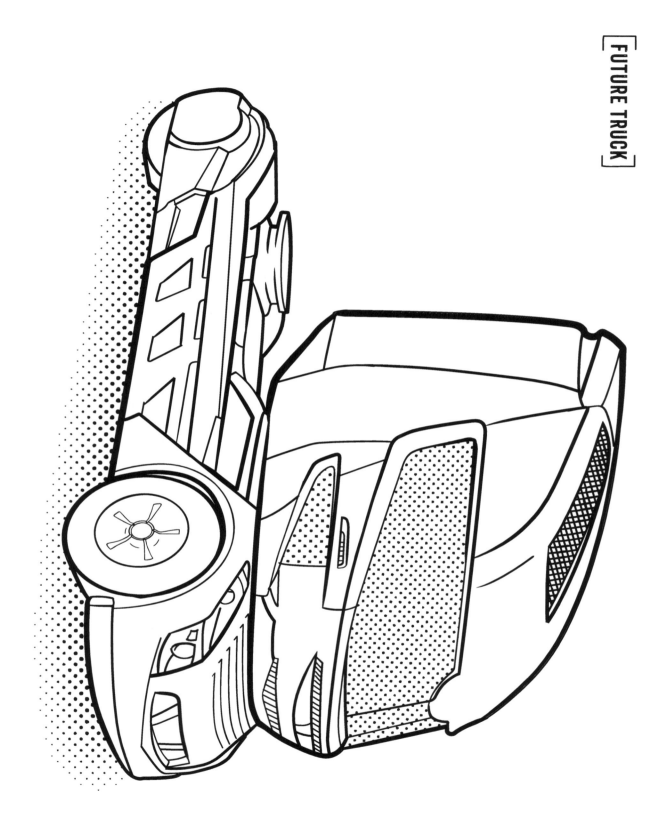

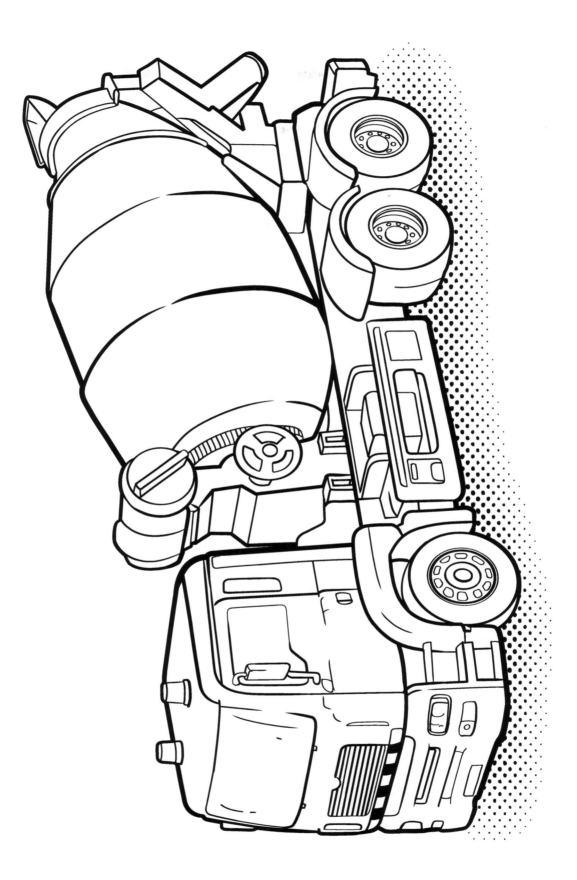

MIXER TRUCK

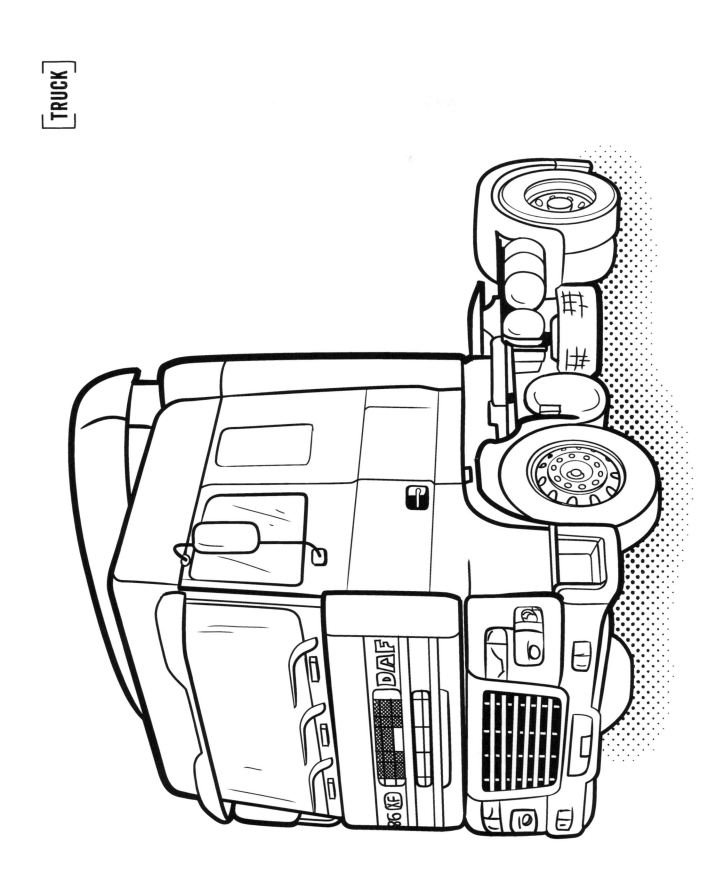

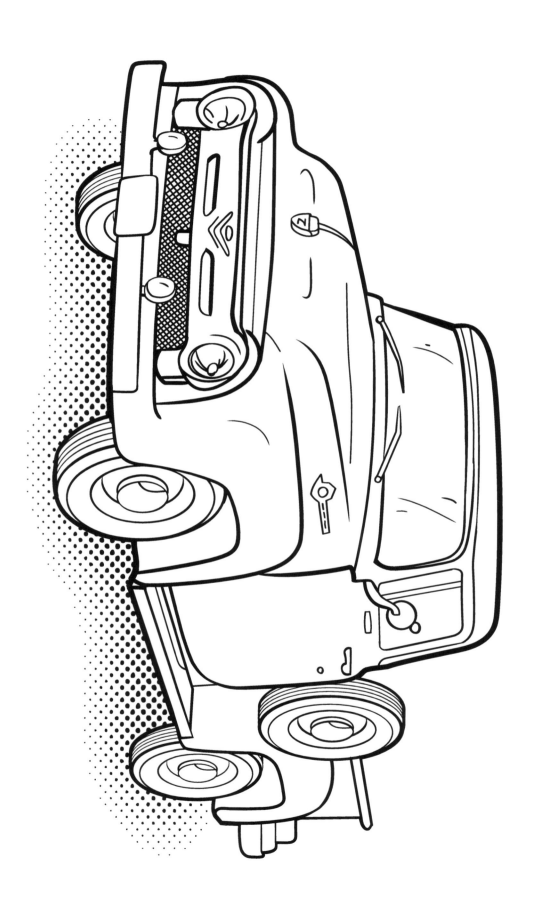

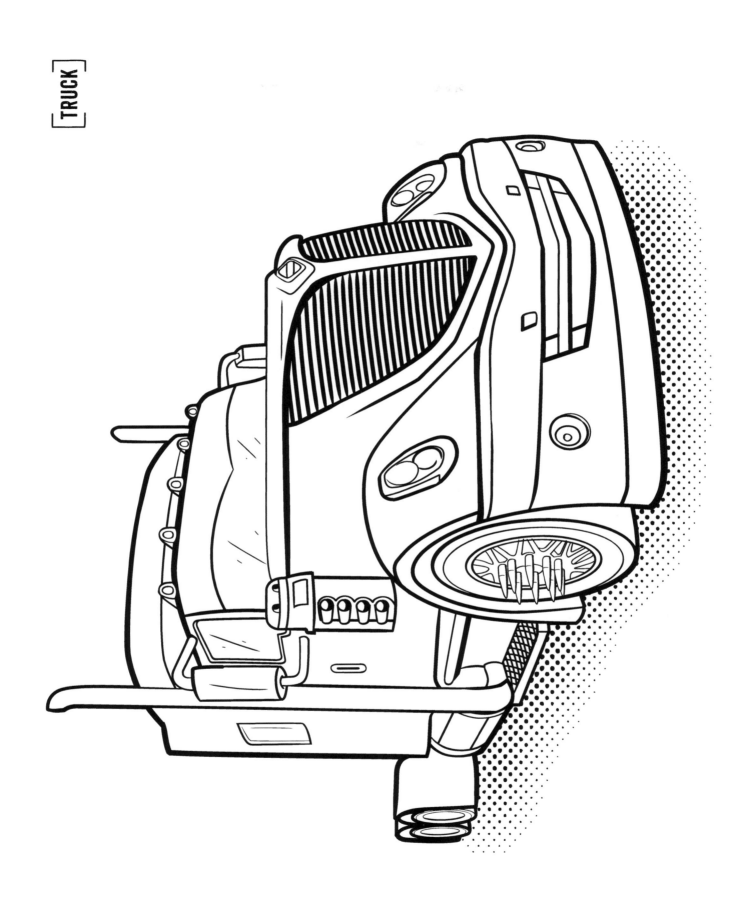

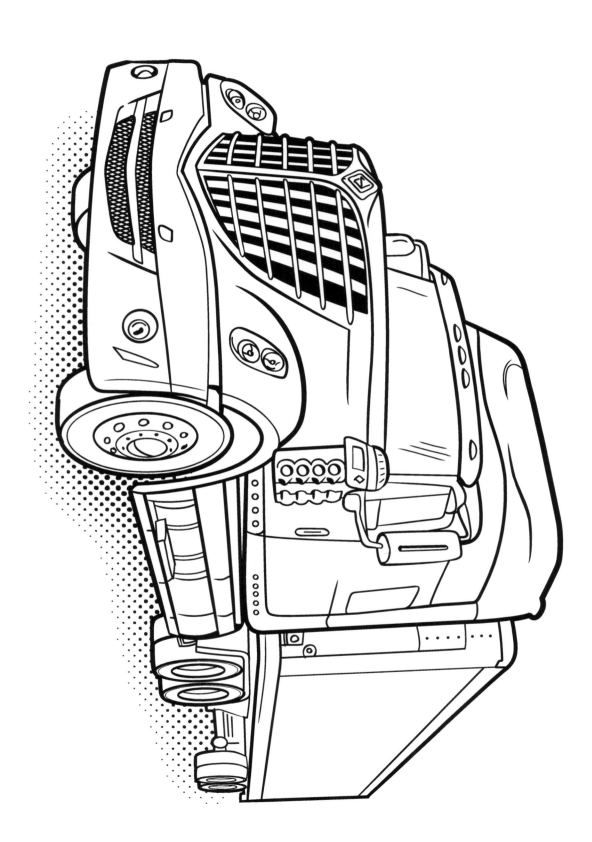

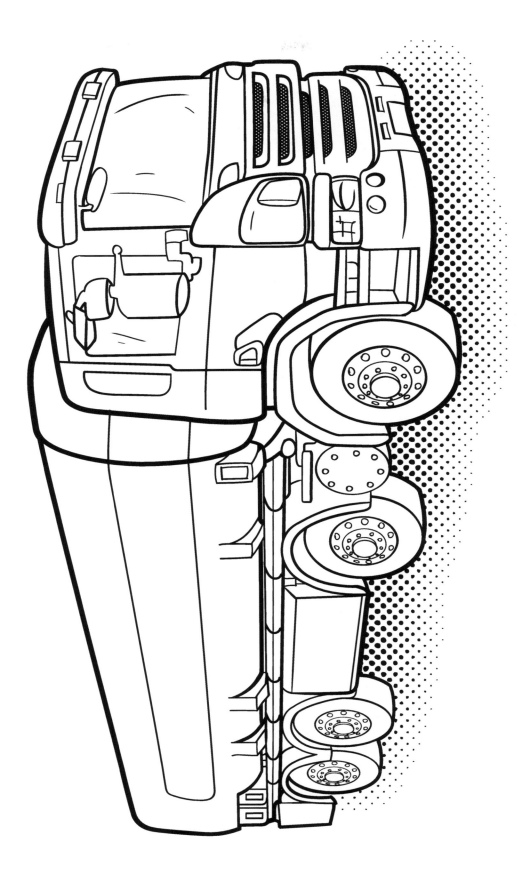

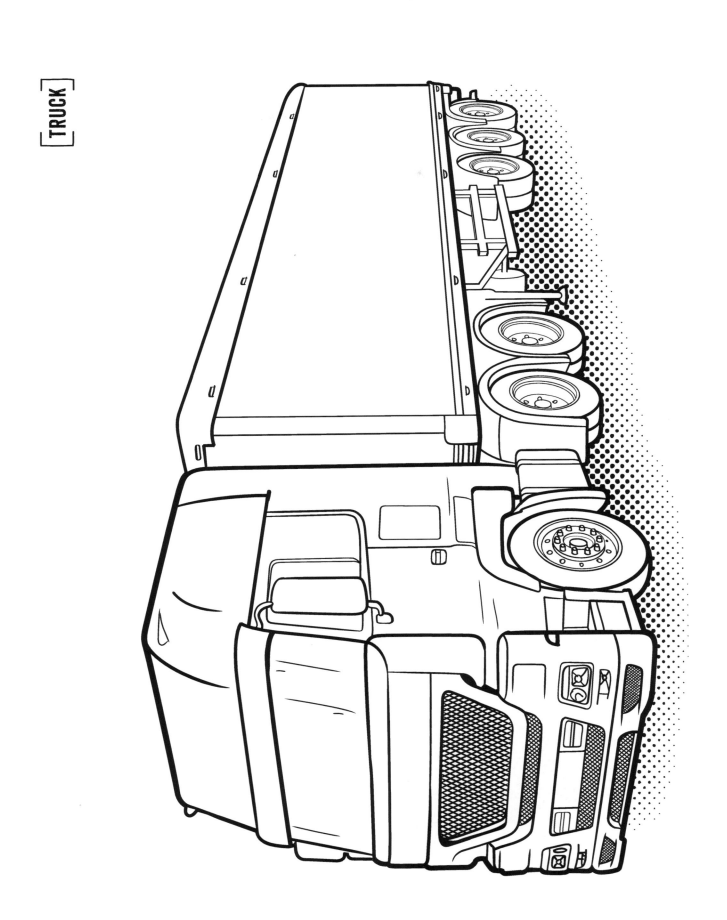

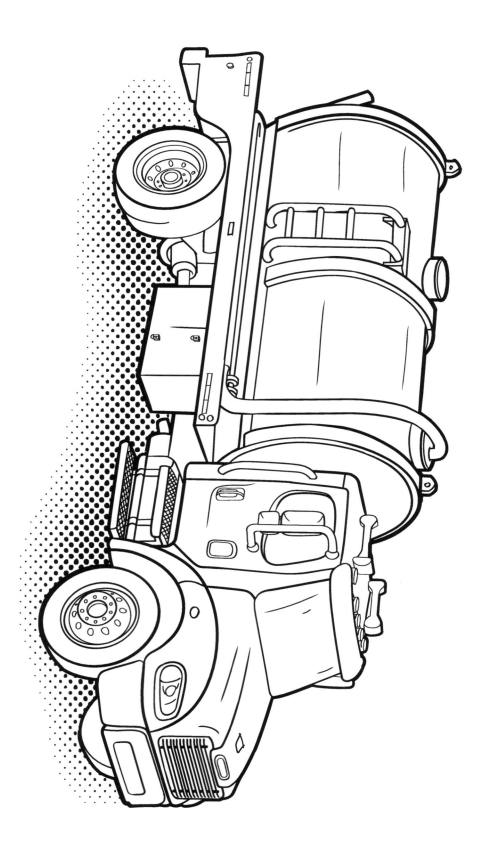

WATER TRUCK

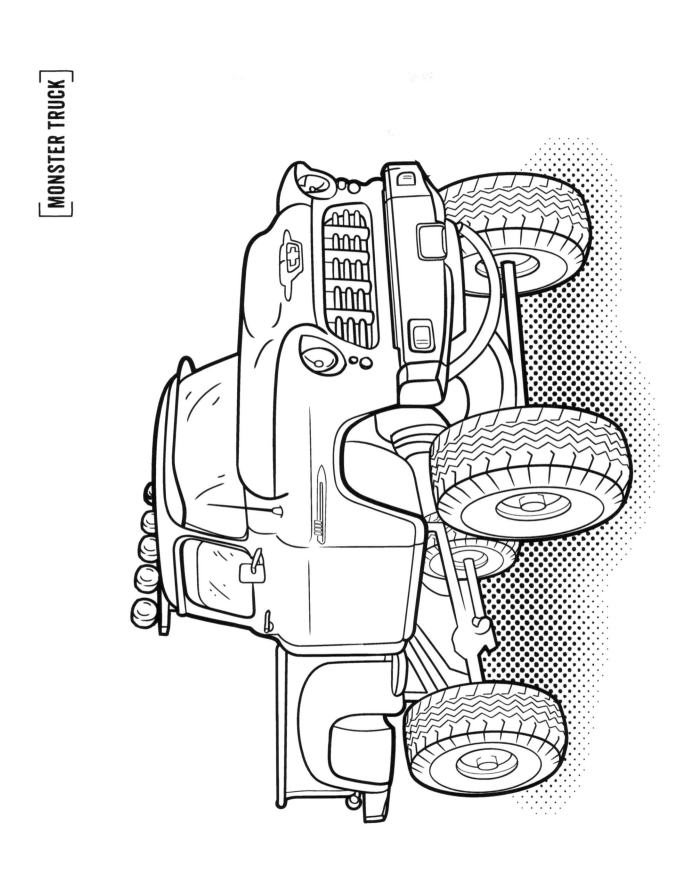

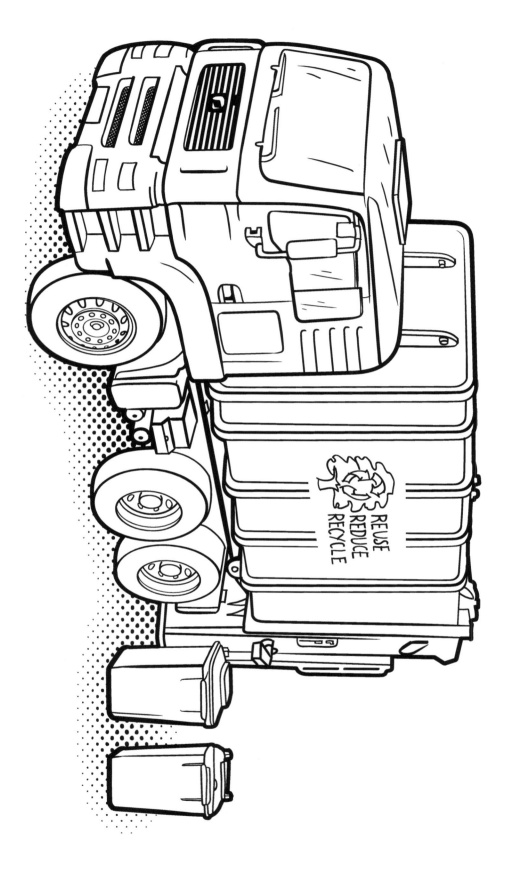

REUSE
REDUCE
RECYCLE

GARBAGE TRUCK

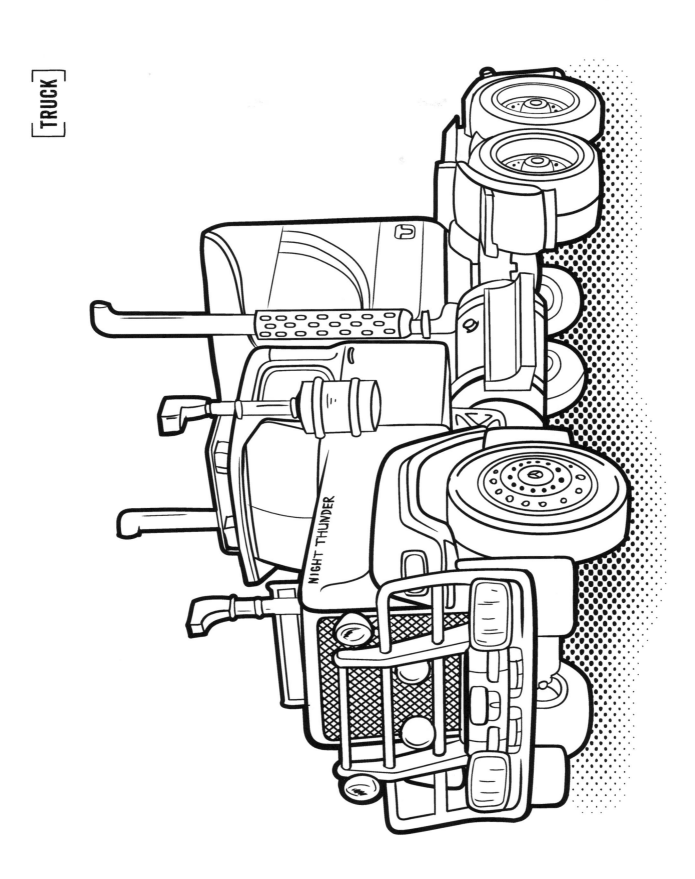

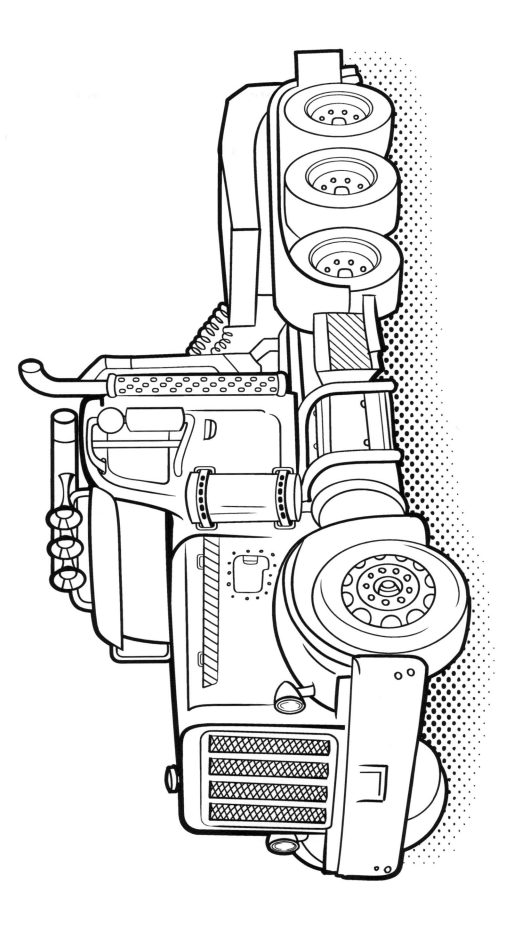

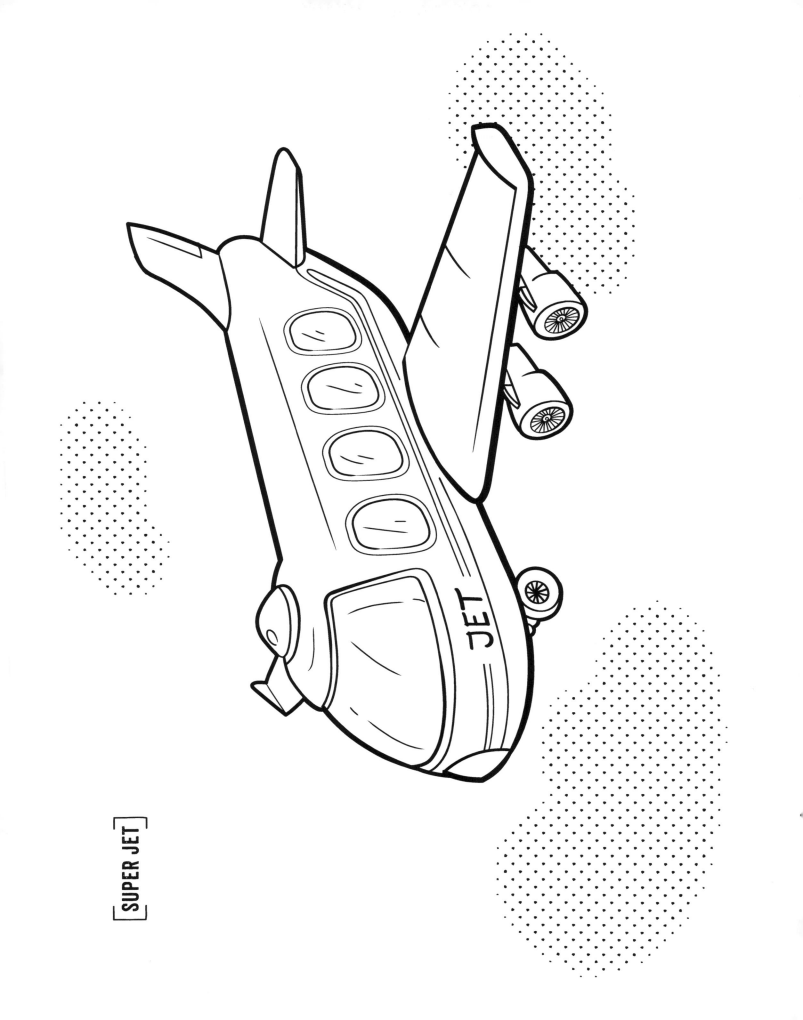

SUPER JET

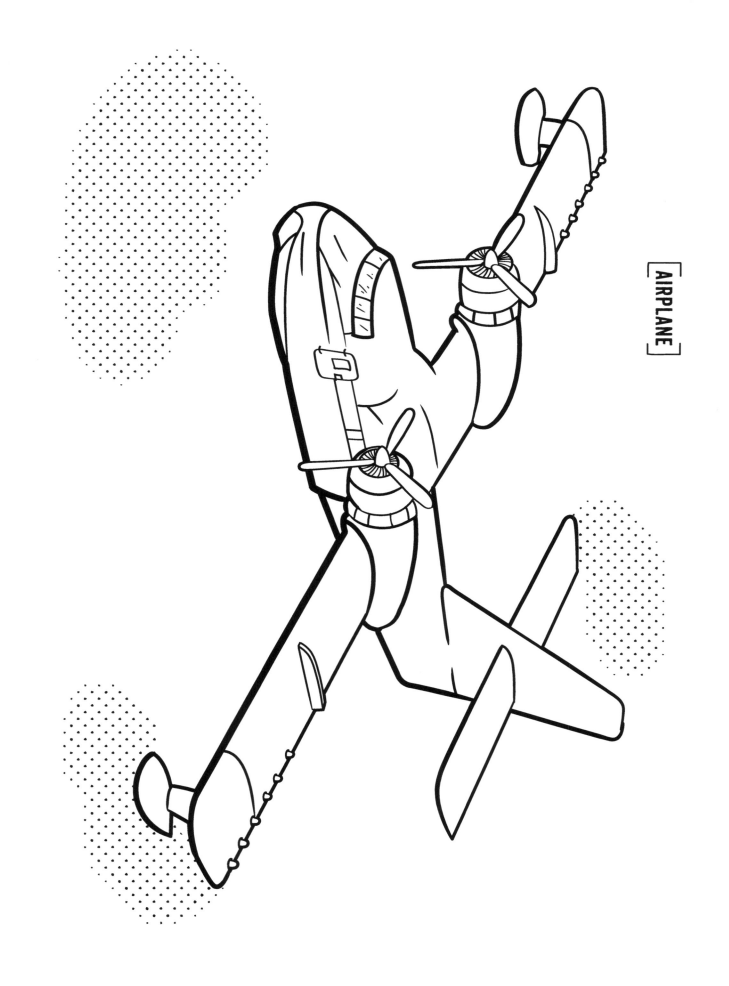

AIRPLANE

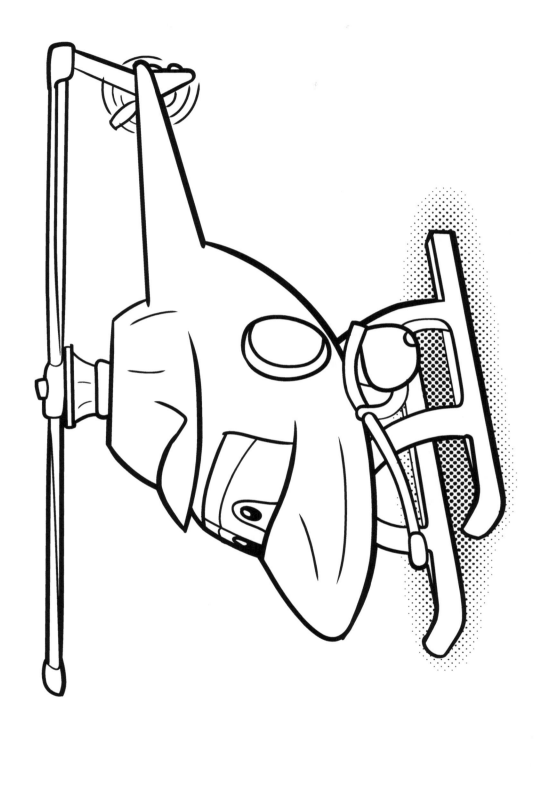

HELICOPTER

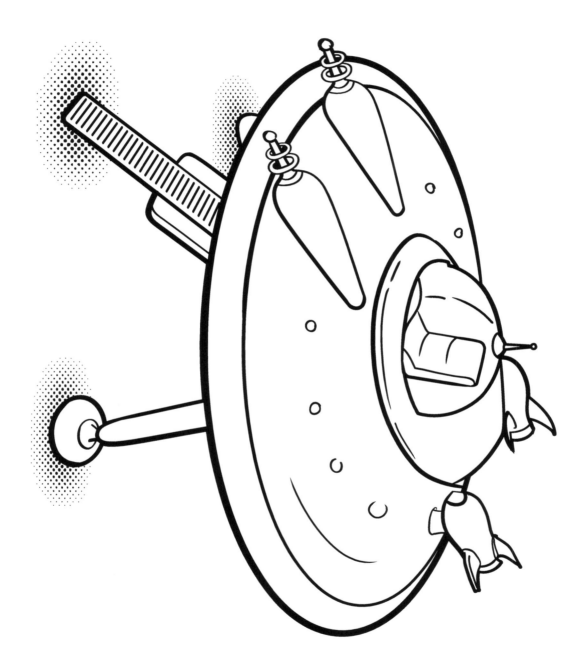

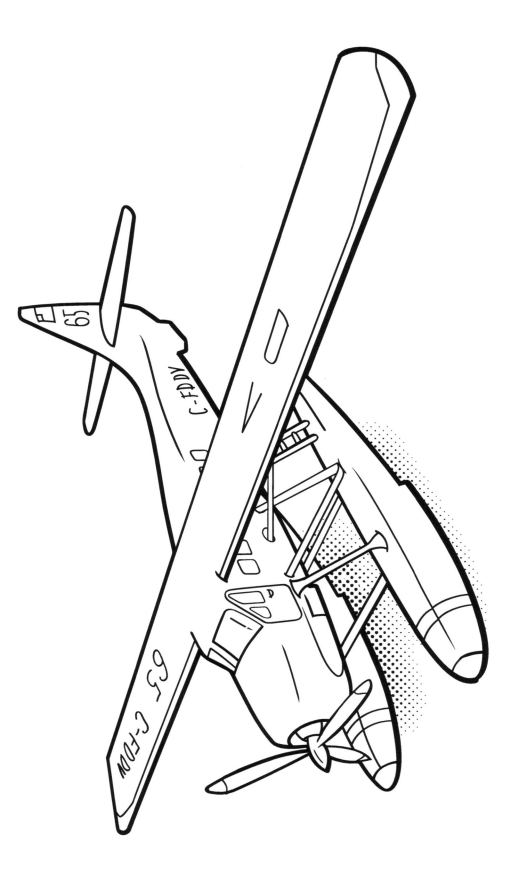

HYDROPLANE

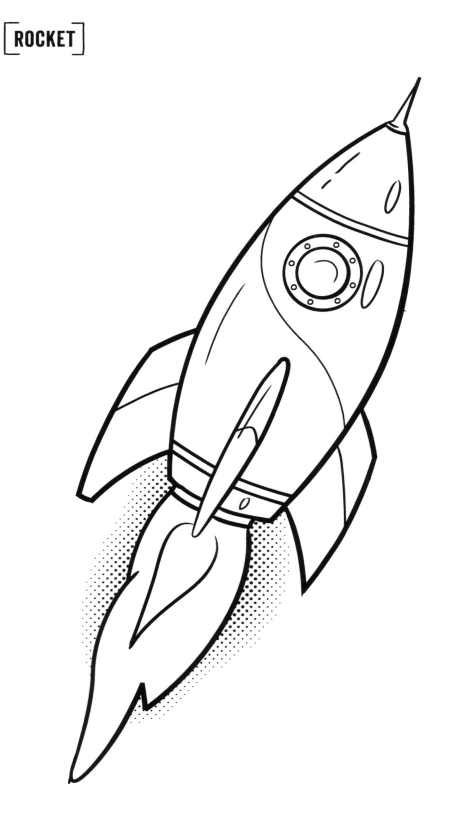

Printed in Poland
by Amazon Fulfillment
Poland Sp. z o.o., Wrocław